PRIDE
POWER

T0321158

PRIDE POWER

Text by Tizzie Frankish.

An Hachette UK Company
www.hachette.co.uk

Vie, an imprint of Summersdale Publishers Ltd
Part of Octopus Publishing Group Limited
Carmelite House
50 Victoria Embankment
LONDON
EC4Y 0DZ
UK

www.summersdale.com

Printed and bound in China

ISBN: 978-1-83799-011-5

Substantial discounts on bulk quantities of Summersdale books are available to corporations, professional associations and other organizations. For details contact general enquiries: telephone: +44 (0) 1243 771107 or email: enquiries@summersdale.com.

PRIDE

POWER

The Young Person's Guide to LGBTQ+

Harriet Dyer

vie

CONTENTS

INTRODUCTION

Hi! Welcome to *Pride Power: A Young Person's Guide to LGBTQ+.*

This introductory guide is not just for those who identify as LGBTQ+; it is for everyone, regardless of gender, identity or ethnicity, and aims to provide greater insight into all things LGBTQ+.

LGBTQ+ culture is rich and diverse and goes all the way back to ancient history. This book will explore the positive changes that have influenced LGBTQ+ culture and show how far queer rights have come. From the hardest struggles to the greatest victories, this book shines a light on the icons and trailblazers who have redefined what it means to be LGBTQ+.

This book includes the most up-to-date thinking on gender, sexuality and identity, and will guide you through some useful terms and phrases – some may be new to you, others you may already know. Throughout the book, you will also find suggestions for other resources for further exploration into the LGBTQ+ culture and community, and links to charities and support groups that you may find useful.

The ABCs of LGBTQ+

It's true that it looks like a bit of a tongue-twister (and getting the letters in the right order is not as easy as it sounds!), but in recent years the original LGBTQ+ term has widened even further to include more identities. It's now a useful umbrella term which covers all non-conforming genders and sexualities and even includes those people who don't want to be assigned to a gender.

So what do the letters stand for?

L = lesbian

G = gay

B = bisexual

T = transgender

Q = questioning or queer (The letter Q can be written twice to represent both)

+ = this symbol represents the wider community within the LGBTQ+ community to include everyone, and to ensure there's room for new language and terminology that better describe identities as language evolves.

You may sometimes see a longer acronym: LGBTQIA2S+. This contains every identity mentioned above, while also adding:

I = intersex

A = asexual

2S = two-spirit, a gender identity used specifically by Native American cultures.

Some people prefer to use the term queer rather than LGBTQ+ because it doesn't name specific identities, while others believe the term queer avoids prioritizing some identities or making reference to the gender/sexuality binary. What do you think?

A note

There are lots of great arguments in favour of using different variations of the acronym, such as LGBTQIA2S+, but for the purposes of ease and quick understanding, LGBTQ+ has been the acronym of choice in this introductory book.

It's always wrong to hate, but never wrong to love.

LADY GAGA

CHAPTER 1

All About Pride

This chapter is all about:

The Pride movement

Celebrating who we are

Raising awareness of the issues faced by the LGBTQ+ community

Exploring the importance of equality and acceptance

9

Pride

Pride means having a deep sense of satisfaction in our own achievements, our values and the way we choose to live. We should all carry a sense of pride in ourselves and support others to feel the same. This is why the Pride movement came into being, because for a long time the LGBTQ+ community has been persecuted for not conforming to traditional expectations of gender and society. The Pride movement embodies acceptance for all genders, and in this chapter, you will discover the true meaning of Pride Power by learning about its beginnings and discover more about the rainbow-coloured celebrations that happen throughout the world every June.

The term 'Pride' was first used in 1967 by a group calling themselves Personal Rights in Defence and Education (PRIDE) who were protesting in Los Angeles against the arrests of their LGBTQ+ patrons. Although the group disbanded, the name was used again years later to embody the Pride movement we know today, which has developed and grown across the world into a big, bright celebration of all things LGBTQ+. The Pride movement has influenced the changing attitudes towards the LGBTQ+ community and the change in laws across the world also represent this. But we still have some way to go for true equality and acceptance.

Change is made one step at a time... Now, let's step up and make a difference, together!

What is Pride?

Pride is a celebration of people coming together in love and friendship, to show how far LGBTQ+ rights have come. It's also an opportunity to shine a light on the areas where there is still work to be done. Every year, usually in June, there are Pride festivals and events held in countries across the world. This month of celebrations, known as Pride Month, marks the anniversary of the Stonewall riots, which began outside the Stonewall Inn, Greenwich Village, New York City, in June 1969.

An American lady called Brenda Howard is known as "The Mother of Pride" after

organizing the first ever gay Pride march on 28 June 1970. However, the suggestion to call the movement "Pride" came from L. Craig Schoonmaker, an activist and member of the New York planning committee. His reasoning was that many people were repressed and did not know how to come out and be proud of who they were. The movement encouraged people to think about who they are and say to themselves, "Maybe I should be proud."

Since the 1970s, Pride events across the world have grown bigger, bolder and, well... prouder!

THE STONEWALL RIOTS

What happened?

In 1969 homosexual relationships were illegal in America (as they were in most countries at that time, although there was partial decriminalization in the UK in 1967). A number of gay bars/taverns opened in New York City as places where gay men, lesbians and transgender people could socialize in safety, away from public persecution. However, these places became targets for harassment from law enforcement.

The Stonewall Inn was a popular gay bar in Greenwich Village that the police raided on 28 June 1969. They arrested the employees for selling liquor without a license and reportedly tried to arrest patrons caught kissing or not wearing gender-appropriate clothing. Frustrated by the police brutality, the patrons didn't flee the scene; they fought back. Lesbians and trans women of colour, including Sylvia Rivera (see page 103) and Marsha P. Johnson, called for reinforcements and barricaded themselves inside the bar, while many onlookers also joined the resistance and around 400 people rioted outside.

What was the outcome?

Five nights of unrest followed. The uprising was seen as a spontaneous protest against the continual police harassment and discrimination suffered by lesbians, gays and transgender people in the 1960s. The Stonewall riot was perhaps the first time that lesbians, gays and transgender people saw past their differences and became united in their fight for a common cause. The riots quickly evolved into an international movement for gay and lesbian rights. Activists celebrated Stonewall's one-year anniversary, which helped raise the profile of the movement, soon to be known as Pride.

LGBTQ+ citizens were no longer prepared to hide or feel shame, and they made themselves visible on the streets and in public spaces with slogans like...

Say it loud, gay is proud!

Why does Pride matter?

People may ask why Pride Month is needed. To those outside the LGBTQ+ community, it might look like Pride isn't necessary any more. However, Pride is a celebration of how far we've come and how far we still have to go in fighting for LGBTQ+ rights around the world. Pride is for EVERYONE... It's a celebration of pride in being yourself, which everyone should celebrate.

Even today Pride plays an important role in:

- **Raising awareness of issues faced by LGBTQ+ people**
- **Creating a safe space for LGBTQ+ people**
- **Building and supporting the community**
- **Encouraging acceptance in the wider community**

Ways to celebrate Pride Month

Pride Month is a wonderful time to recognize the achievements of the LGBTQ+ community, learn about LGBTQ+ history, celebrate diversity and contribute to creating a more inclusive society. So, what can you do to be part of Pride? There are a number of things beyond attending Pride parades or events, such as:

- **Support LGBTQ+ arts and culture by visiting LGBTQ+ art galleries and creative spaces**

- **Donate to an LGBTQ+ charity (charities listed in Chapter 5)**

- **Organize a Pride awareness activity in school or in your community, such**

Ally
Allyship means you're doing the hard work to actively support people from marginalized groups.

as T-shirt designing or creating a flag (see Chapter 3 for flag inspiration)

- Consider your school/college's LGBTQ+ inclusivity culture and resources – ask if LGBTQ+ space can be created on your school website or classroom walls where you can include LGBTQ+ information, resources and events, and suggest inclusive books and films for your school library (for further information, see Chapter 5)

- Be an ally and/or an advocate – there are details on how you might do this in Chapter 5

Advocate

Advocacy is taking action in service of a cause and the people it affects to influence decision makers and decision-making.

Pride is not just for June... it's all year round!

WHAT DOES ACCEPTANCE LOOK LIKE?

LGBTQ+ acceptance is the same as any other form of social acceptance, but it specifically relates to how society reacts to, supports and values people who identify as LGBTQ+.

Social acceptance

1. the formal or informal admission of an individual into a group.

2. the absence of social disapproval.

For LGBTQ+ individuals

It is about feeling loved and valued by friends and family. It's about feeling safe to be/show who you are at home and school and feeling like an equal member of society.

For the LGBTQ+ community

It's about political and economic empowerment, where there is equal access and opportunity for all. A person's LGBTQ+ identity should not stop them from gaining employment, being promoted at work or being a valued member of society.

For those who don't identify as LGBTQ+

It's about accepting and celebrating the diversity of your friends, family and peers. It's about finding ways to help prevent LGBTQ+ discrimination and to challenge it when you see it. It's about becoming an ally and advocate for the LGBTQ+ community.

HOW DOES BIAS IMPACT LGBTQ+ ACCEPTANCE?

Whether we even realize it, we all have unconscious biases. How a person thinks can depend on their life experiences, and biases are often created by our surroundings, from childhood experiences, from the TV shows/films we watch, the social media we use and even from the books we read. As a result, individuals may have beliefs and views about other people that might not be right or reasonable... and it's important to check and explore our biases so we don't unknowingly discriminate against those who identify as LGBTQ+ (or anyone else in society, for that matter!).

Unconscious bias

These are social stereotypes about certain groups of people that individuals form outside of their own conscious awareness.

It's important to think about your own biases and find ways to understand and manage them. You might do this by:

Being conscious of assumptions you make about someone who identifies as LGBTQ+. What thoughts do you have on their lifestyle or preferences?

Engaging with LGBTQ+ media, such as following LGBTQ+ political news and watching TV shows and films and reading books with positive LGBTQ+ representation.

Being curious and finding ways to understand the challenges that the LGBTQ+ community face. You can do this by asking genuine questions and really listening to the answers (see Chapter 5 on how to be a better listener). Joining in LGBTQ+ events in your local area or organizing one yourself.

Remember, PRIDE is for EVERYONE.

Equality for all...

The LGBTQ+ community want equal rights, not special rights. However, in many countries, discrimination based on sexual orientation and gender identity is still legal. There are places where a person can be kicked out of school, fired from a job or denied housing because of who they love or how they express their gender. A number of years after same-sex marriage was legalized in the UK, the majority of Western Europe (excluding Italy), Australia and the USA, basic freedoms are still missing in 29 states for LGBTQ+ Americans. More than half of the countries around the world that allow same-sex marriage are in Europe, and there are still more than 30 countries around the world where same-sex marriage is illegal.

Right now what matters is that you guys know that no matter who you love, that it's okay and that it's awesome and the world is there for you.

JOJO SIWA

CHANGING ATTITUDES AND ACCEPTANCE

The good news is that around the world, LGBTQ+ acceptance is increasing and the global divide over LGBTQ+ rights is narrowing.

These are the top ten countries where people responded "yes, homosexuality should be accepted by society"*

1 Sweden (94%)

2 Netherlands (92%)

3 Spain (89%)

26

4
France (86%)

5
Germany (86%)

6
UK (86%)

7
Canada (85%)

8
Australia (81%)

9
Argentina (76%)

10
Italy (75%)

*survey conducted among 38,426 people in 34 countries from 13 May to 2 October 2019 Pew Research Center, June 2020, "The Global Divide on Homosexuality Persists"

Misconceptions about the LGBTQ+ community:

The LGBTQ+ community is "shoving their personal business and beliefs in people's faces".

If young people are around or brought up by individuals who identify as LGBTQ+, it will "turn them that way" too.

Response:

If it's okay for straight people to show public displays of affection (PDA), then everyone else should be able to do this too.

If being LGBTQ+ is not part of who an individual is to begin with, nothing is going to "turn" them. Being LGBTQ+ is an innate part of who you are.

THERE'S STILL WORK TO DO!

Despite all the progress being made on acceptance and equality for the LGBTQ+ community, there are still issues which affect many young people.

In school

When a person struggles with differences in others, it can sometimes result in them engaging in bullying behaviours. The bullying may take the form of name-calling, spreading rumours, cyberbullying or physical or emotional abuse. This can happen both in the classroom and on social media.

Although there has been a drive for LGBTQ+ inclusivity in schools across the world, there has been a push back against this from parents and some school staff.

At home

Some young people face challenges and obstacles when family members disagree with their LGBTQ+ identity. In extreme cases, young people have been rejected by their families altogether.

In the community

Many LGBTQ+ people fear going out in public with their partners and showing affection towards them, such as by holding hands or kissing in public. Sadly, there are still instances where members of the LGBTQ+ community have been attacked for doing just this.

Supportive LGBTQ+ organizations

If you, your friends or LGBTQ+ peers are experiencing any issues related to LGBTQ+ identity, please talk to a trusted adult. Wherever you are in the world, there are young people's services and support groups nationally, regionally and possibly in your local area. A quick internet search will confirm this, but here is a list of organizations that might be useful:

Young people's services and support groups

akt.org.uk	**mosaictrust.org.uk**
allsortsyouth.org.uk	**outreachyouth.org.uk**
diversitytrust.org.uk/young-peoples-services	**pridesports.org.uk/pride-youth-games**
gaycenter.org	**qalliance.org.uk**
iglyo.com	**sayit.org.uk**
justlikeus.org	**theproudtrust.org**
lgbtyouth.org.uk	**thetrevorproject.org**
metrocharity.org.uk/youth	**ypapride.org**
ypapride.org	**belongto.org**

Further resources such as forums and charities can be found in Chapter 5.

CHAPTER 2

What's in a Name? Labels and Definitions

This chapter is all about:

The difference between sex and gender

The definitions of gender and sexuality

Pride flags

Sex is not gender and gender is not sex!

Say what? Aren't sex and gender the same thing? Spoiler alert... No!

"Sex" and "gender" tend to be understood as meaning the same thing, so it's easy to get them muddled up.

Sex is a scientific term relating to biology and where humans are categorized into two sexes, male and female. A person's sex is designed by a set of physical characteristics, including genitals, sex organs and hormones.

Society's understanding of biological sex has changed over time, and new information suggests that the idea of only two sexes in humans is possibly too simplistic.

Gender can be defined by biological sex, gender roles and gender identity. One or all of these factors may define a person's gender, depending on their own gender expression.*

*this is explored in further detail on pages 44-48.

Perhaps the easiest way to explain it is with this diagram.

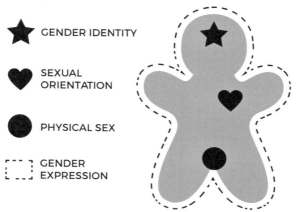

★ GENDER IDENTITY

♥ SEXUAL ORIENTATION

● PHYSICAL SEX

⌐ ¬ GENDER EXPRESSION

Genderbread diagram

This infographic helpfully shows that sex is of the body and gender is of the mind. Sex is usually categorized for humans as male, female and intersex. An intersex person is born with sex characteristics that do not wholly belong in either category of male or female. This can include:

- ambiguous genitalia

- smaller than expected male genitalia

- larger than expected female genitalia

- delayed or absent puberty or unexpected puberty changes

35

Gender: a social system of classification

Gender can be defined by several factors: biological sex, social structures such as gender roles (the way society expects men and women to act and behave) and gender identity. Gender classification is historically rooted in the ideas society has about males and females, and most gender identities are based around these. However, society is starting to recognize gender identities that reject masculinity and femininity and stand outside of the binary.

Society

A large group of people living together in an organized way, who make decisions about how to do things and share the work that needs to be done, such as people in a country or in several similar countries.

Binary

Consisting of two things or parts or involving a choice between two alternatives only (such as on-off or yes-no).

Gender roles

Male and female gender roles are defined by the way society expects males and females to act. These expectations can include how people present themselves both in physical appearance and personality and can also influence the hobbies they choose and the jobs they hope to do. For example, can you sort the following list into traditional masculine or feminine attributes?

- Long hair
- Big muscles
- Loud
- Funny
- Quiet

- Gentle
- Primary care giver
- Doctor
- Dancer
- Footballer

Easy, right? Or not so much?

Society is changing... slowly! But it is changing, and the answers you gave may be different to your parents'/guardians', which will be different again to their parents'/guardians'.

Gender expression

Gender expression is how a person chooses to display or express their gender identity. Society is a strange beast... When you think about it, doesn't it seem odd that almost everything you do, say or wear is a form of gender expression? Certain haircuts and whether a person wears make-up or not are unofficially categorized as masculine or feminine, as is the way a person walks and talks and the gestures they use. Even some jobs are seen to be more suited to one gender than another. But times are changing, and people are realizing that they don't have to stick to the gender bias that tradition dictates.

Maybe I'm not a man, maybe I'm not a woman, maybe I'm just me.

SAM SMITH

Gender pronouns

Tiny but mighty, pronouns are the essential building blocks for effective and respectful communication. However, in the English language, many pronouns are gendered, which is totally NOT helpful if an individual identifies outside of the gender binary.

Pronoun

A word that takes the place of a noun. Common examples are:
I, me, he, him, she, her, you, we, they, them.

For some people, neither him nor her represents their gender, and you can't always tell what pronouns someone uses just by looking at them. But there are ways around this. One is using gender-neutral pronouns like they and them to replace he/she and him/her. The best option, when you do not know a person's gender, is simply to ask. It is perfectly acceptable to ask someone what pronouns they use and use their name until you learn their pronouns.

If in doubt... ask!

The easiest way to ask someone about their pronouns is to share your own:

"Hello, my name is Charlie, and I go by 'he, him, his' pronouns."

By using your pronouns, you are showing that you are familiar with the concept of pronouns and are respectful of them, which is particularly important if you are speaking to a member of the LGBTQ+ community. You could also add:

"What pronouns do you use?"

Both these suggestions create the opportunity for the other person to share their pronouns in their introduction. It shows you are an ally and it normalizes the sharing of pronouns in public spaces and/or interactions. So it might be a bit awkward the first few times you do this, but it does get easier. Promise!

Ally

Being an ally means offering unconditional kindness without judgment of another's life experiences. Let's face it; this should apply to all human beings.

You can find more information on what it means to be an LGBTQ+ ally and advice on advocacy and activism in Chapter 5.

LABELS

Labels... Everyone loves them. From designer to high street, and even labels for people. But here's the thing... labelling people doesn't always work that well. You know why? Mislabelling. Queer people are often mislabelled, just because someone else doesn't understand their identity. But it's not fair, and it's not okay. If people are going to label, they need to get it right. Right? Queer people can be empowered by labels. It can be a strong and affirming act to name yourself using a term that tells the world, "I am one of many". It is also empowering to have a symbol or a queer pride flag that represents the group with which you identify.

This chapter will fly the flag for the many gender identities and sexual orientations. Just like the identities, each and every flag is different and has a right to be celebrated. Alongside the definitions, there are flags of all colours and combinations and a brief explanation of how they evolved from the original Gilbert Baker Pride Flag, which was the brainchild of Harvey Milk, in 1977.

Now, let's go wave those flags...

GENDER LABELS

Gender neutral

If a person describes themselves as gender neutral, it means they do not identify as one gender more than any other gender.

"Gender neutral" is also used to refer to something which is not about or intended for one gender over another. Gender neutrality is useful in all sorts of ways. One example is where it has been used in job titles, such as fire officer instead of firewoman or fireman. Another is not segregating toys by gender and allowing children to choose the toys they want to play with. The #Lettoysbetoys hashtag on social media encouraged discussion and was instrumental in shining a light on gendered toys such as blue Lego for boys and pink for girls. Seriously, LET TOYS JUST BE TOYS!

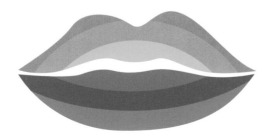

Gender-fluid/ gender flexible

A person who is gender-fluid/gender flexible has no fixed identity within the gender spectrum. Their identity is fluid and is able and likely to change – which might occur from one day to the next, or they may feel differently from week to week or month to month. The person's identity might be focussed on one area of the gender spectrum, or it may move freely between completely different identities. Remember, the fluidity of an identity can be felt at any time.

Third Gender

A person who does not identify as male or female, but as neither, both, or a combination of male and female genders.

Gender-fluid/Gender Flexible Pride Flag

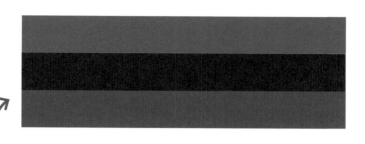

The gender-fluid flag was created by JJ Poole, an agender pansexual, in 2012. The colours represent the whole spectrum of gender. The pink stands for femininity and the blue stands for masculinity, with purple symbolizing a combination of the two. White is associated with lack of gender and the black represents all genders, including third genders.

Transgender

An umbrella term to describe people whose gender is not the same as, or does not sit comfortably with, the sex they were assigned at birth. As gender is an internal experience and not a person's sex characteristics, someone might identify as transgender and have only partial or no surgery to alter their sex characteristics.

Transgender or trans people may describe themselves using one or more of a wide variety of terms, including (but not limited to) transgender, transsexual, gender-queer (GQ), gender-fluid, non-binary, trans man, trans woman, trans masculine, trans feminine and neutrois.

Transgender man

Someone who is assigned female at birth but identifies and lives as a man. This may be shortened to trans man, or FTM, an abbreviation for female-to-male.

Transgender woman

Someone who is assigned male at birth but identifies and lives as a woman. This may be shortened to trans woman, or MTF, an abbreviation for male-to-female.

Transgender Pride Flag

Monica Helms, a trans woman, designed this flag in 1999. The light blue is the traditional colour for baby boys, the pink is for girls and the white in the middle is for those who are transitioning or identify as neutral gender or no gender, and those who are intersex.

Neutrois

A person who has a neutral gender identity or who lacks a specific gender identity.

Agender

This is used to refer to someone who does not identify as any particular gender. Other terms that have a similar meaning to agender include gender-neutral or neutrois. A person who identifies as agender does not identify with any gender identity on the gender spectrum, including male and female. They may choose to use gender-neutral pronouns, so remember: if in doubt... ask!

Cisgender

A cisgender person is one whose assigned-at-birth sex matches their gender identity. By saying cisgender, instead of what may have previously been labelled as the default gender or "normal", it acknowledges that everyone has a relationship between their birth gender and gender identification.

A commonly used abbreviation for cisgender is "cis".

Agender Pride Flag

Designed by artist and activist Salem Fontana, the agender flag was unveiled on the social media platform Tumblr in 2014. The black and white stripes represent the absence of gender, while green, the inverse of the gender-heavy purple, represents non-binary genders.

NOT A PHASE

Intersex

An intersex person is one who is born with sex characteristics that do not wholly belong to male or female. Some intersex babies are assigned a gender at birth and raised as that gender; some may later assign their own gender, while others continue to identify as that gender. It is important to note that there is no right or wrong in this instance; it's about individual choice.

LOVE IS LOVE

Intersex Pride Flag

Designed in 2013 by the organization
Intersex International Australia, this
flag intentionally features non-gendered
colours that celebrate living outside the
binary. The flag's colours and symbols
"seek to completely avoid anything to
do with gender" and the purple circle
"symbolizes wholeness, completeness and our
potentialities", according to the designer,
Morgan Carpenter.

Non-binary

A non-binary person is someone who is not defined by a system of identification involving only two genders.

Of the gender and sexual identities included in this book, the ones that are most well-known involve a binary choice: male or female, gay or straight. Non-binary identities are those that exist beyond the binary options and include identities that are neither, a little bit or a combination of these things. Gender-fluid is one example of a non-binary identity. Can you think of any others?

BORN
THIS
WAY

Non-Binary Pride Flag

Created in 2014 by 17-year-old Kye Rowan, who identifies as a non-binary person, this flag was a response to non-binary people feeling improperly represented by the genderqueer flag. The yellow symbolizes gender outside a binary. The white, a mix of all colours, represents those with many or all genders. Purple stands in for those who feel both binary male and female or fluid between them. The black is for the agender community, without sexuality or colour.

SEXUALITY AND SEXUAL ORIENTATION

Sexuality is how individuals express themselves romantically and/or sexually.

It is not really known what shapes individual sexuality. Although we can choose whether to act on our feelings, psychologists do not consider sexual orientation to be a conscious choice that can be voluntarily changed.

So, you see, our sexuality is a natural part of who we are, and it's different for everyone. For many people, it is clear from a young age the gender(s) they are attracted to, but for others, this can be harder to define. All of the above is perfectly normal... it is perfectly YOU!

As we go through puberty, hormones affect our bodies and emotions in new ways. This makes us curious about sex and more likely to have sexual thoughts and feelings, but this can develop at different times for individuals. The age of consent in most countries around the world is 16 (however, this age may vary from state to state in America/Australia and may be higher in some countries). This is the age when young people of any sex, gender or sexual orientation can legally consent to take part in sexual activity.

Just like gender, there are many different terms used to describe sexuality, and this section explores those most commonly used, although they may be subject to change. Please remember, if an individual identifies their sexuality with a term not included here, it does not make it any less valid. This list is by no means exhaustive. For a wider list of LGBTQ+ terms please refer to https://www. stonewall.org.uk/list-lgbtq-terms.

Gender and sexuality are so fluid. It's OK to change your mind a million times and figure out what works for you. It's OK to take your time.

Amandla Stenberg

SEXUAL ORIENTATION LABELS

Queer

Those who reject specific labels of romantic orientation, sexual orientation and/or gender identity use the term queer. They may use the term to identify all these aspects of their identity or just the individual aspects. For example, they may identify as queer with regards to their gender identity, but gay in their sexual orientation. Although some LGBTQ+ people view the word as a slur, in the 1980s it was reclaimed and embraced by the queer community.

GAY PRIDE

is loading

Gilbert Baker Pride Flag

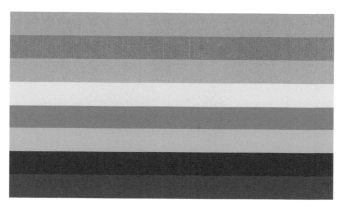

In 1977, Harvey Milk challenged American artist, designer and activist Gilbert Baker to come up with a symbol of pride for the gay community. The original Pride flag, inspired by a song in The Wizard of Oz, sung by Judy Garland, "Over the Rainbow", celebrates every aspect of queer Pride with a colour:

Hot pink   =   Sex
Red   =   Life
Orange   =   Healing
Yellow   =   Sunlight
Green   =   Nature
Turquoise   =   Magic/Art
Indigo   =   Serenity
Violet   =   Spirit

Traditional Gay Pride Flag

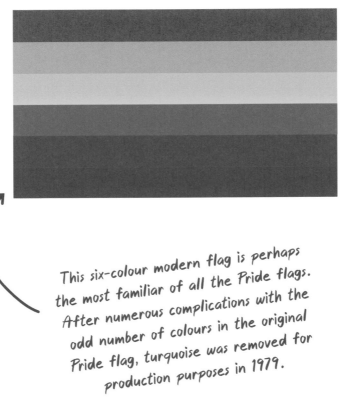

This six-colour modern flag is perhaps the most familiar of all the Pride flags. After numerous complications with the odd number of colours in the original Pride flag, turquoise was removed for production purposes in 1979.

Progress Pride Flag

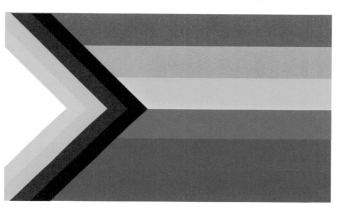

Created in 2018 by non-binary artist Daniel Quasar, the Progress Pride flag is based on the iconic 1978 rainbow flag. It has additional stripes of black and brown to represent marginalized LGBTQ+ people of colour as well as the triad of blue, pink and white from the trans flag, and the design represents diversity and inclusion.

Lesbian

A woman who has a romantic and/or sexual attraction to other women. Some non-binary people may also identify with this term.

Lesbian Pride Flag

In an effort to be more inclusive, the pink and purple flag was redesigned in 2018. Using the lipstick lesbian flag as a starting point, the updated version includes shades of orange. The colours in this modern lesbian flag represent:

Darkest Orange: Gender non-conformity
Middle Orange: Independence
Lightest Orange: Community
White: Unique relationships to womanhood
Lightest Pink: Serenity and peace
Middle Pink: Love and sex
Darkest Pink: Femininity

Homosexual

This is a traditional term used to describe someone who has a romantic and/or sexual orientation towards someone of the same gender. The term "gay" is now more generally used; however, some people still prefer "homosexual" to any other term.

Gay

A term used to refer to a man who has a romantic and/or sexual orientation towards men. However, it is now used as a generic term for lesbian and gay sexuality – some women define themselves as gay rather than lesbian. Some non-binary people may also identify with this term.

One of the reasons in favour of using the word queer as an umbrella term over gay is that the term gay used to relate to males and their experiences. However, in recent years, the term has become much broader and inclusive of the female experience. The Dictionary. com definition defines it as "relating to, or exhibiting sexual desire or behaviour directed toward people of one's own sex or gender".

The Gay Men's Pride Flag

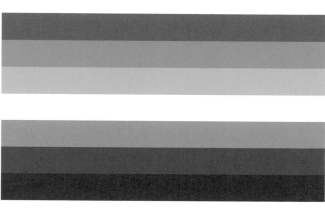

The Gay Men's Pride Flag features different shades of green, blue and purple and is a revamp of an earlier flag that featured a range of blue tones (and was problematic because it used traditional colours of the male gender binary). This updated flag is much more inclusive as it is not limited to transgender, intersex and gender nonconforming men.

Bisexual (Bi)

This term describes sexual attraction towards people of the same gender as well as people of other genders.

Some people see the "bi' in bisexual as assuming that gender is binary (a choice between two options) and includes only two genders, which they believe erases the experience of people who identify as genderqueer or non-binary. However, many people that identify as bisexual do recognize genderqueer/non-binary identities, but bisexual is simply the term they feel most comfortable identifying as.

Bisexual Pride Flag

Designed by bisexual activist Michael Page in 1998, the flag brings visibility to the bisexual community, showing the overlap of the stereotypical colours for boys and girls. The flag was inspired by an older symbol of bisexuality: the "biangles", which consisted of two overlapping pink and dark blue triangles.

Pansexual

This refers to a person whose romantic and/or sexual attraction towards others is not limited by sex or gender.

At first glance, the definition of pansexual is similar to that of bisexual; however, bisexuality generally refers to an attraction to more than one gender, and pansexuality is defined as attraction to someone regardless of gender. People's definitions of bisexuality and pansexuality might vary, and ultimately, it's personal choice when it comes to the language an individual chooses to identify themselves.

Pansexual Pride Flag

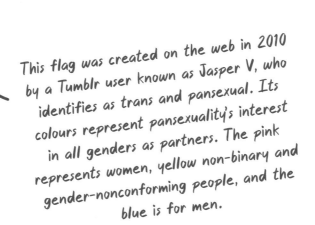

This flag was created on the web in 2010 by a Tumblr user known as Jasper V, who identifies as trans and pansexual. Its colours represent pansexuality's interest in all genders as partners. The pink represents women, yellow non-binary and gender-nonconforming people, and the blue is for men.

Heterosexual

This is commonly used as an umbrella term for cisgender individuals who express a preference for romantic and/or sexual relationships with people of a different cisgender; when a man is attracted to a woman and vice versa.

As we already know from earlier chapters, gender identity describes a person's internal, personal sense of being a man or a woman, or someone outside of the gender binary, and sexual orientation describes a person's physical, romantic and/or emotional attraction to another person (for example: heterosexual, gay, lesbian, bisexual). Therefore, some transgender people identify as heterosexual. For example, a person who transitions from male to female and is only attracted to men may identify as a straight woman. Equally, a person who is heterosexual may also be attracted to someone who is a transgender person.

A slang term for heterosexual includes "straight", a term that is now commonly used for people who have identified as heterosexual all their lives.

Straight Ally Pride Flag

Sometimes known as the *Ally Pride Flag*, this is a combination of different symbols – the straight flag is black and white stripes, the traditional pride flag is a rainbow – and the combination is meant to show allyship for the LGBTQ+ community.

Asexual

A term used for someone who does not usually feel sexual attraction and/or a sexual urge towards other people. Asexuality works on a spectrum, like sexuality; some people who consider themselves to be asexual never feel sexual attraction or urges; others do on occasion.

Remember, just like puberty, people's sexual attraction develops at different times, so it's okay to take time to work things out. If you don't feel sexual attraction to anyone, it might not mean you are asexual; it might mean those thoughts and feelings are yet to develop. Equally, if you feel that describing yourself as asexual is helpful to you, then that's okay too.

Demisexual

A word used to describe a person who may only feel sexually attracted to people with whom they have formed an emotional bond. People may also use terms such as gay, bi, lesbian, straight and queer in conjunction with demi to explain the direction of romantic or sexual attraction as they experience it.

Asexual Pride Flag

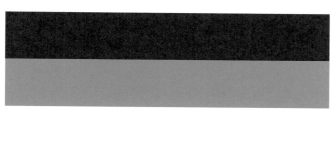

Like the pansexual flag, the asexual flag was created in 2010. Inspired by the Asexual Visibility and Education Network logo, it represents many asexual identities. The asexuality flag has four colours: purple represents community, white represents non-asexual allies and partners, grey represents demisexuality and black represents asexuality.

Questioning

This refers to anyone who is unsure of and/or is exploring their own sexual orientation and/or gender identity. A person can be questioning at any age.

The teenage years are the time when individuals discover important parts of their identity, and this can include sexual orientation and/or gender identity. If someone feels uncertainty about this and it is causing distress, it is important to talk to an adult they can trust. (There are also helpful resources and practical advice in Chapter 5.)

Everyone has the right to be themselves without needing to explain this to anyone. Feeling pressure to hide who you are can feel stressful and affect your mental and physical well-being over time. For many people, understanding their sexuality and being themselves is usually relieving, freeing and exciting! But there is no specific time that this "should" happen – for some people sexual identity develops over a period of time, and for others it may be more immediate. If labels are helpful to you, then use them. Likewise, if they aren't, then don't use them. Your sexuality = your choice on how you do or don't define it!

All I gotta say is follow your gut and don't feel like you owe any sort of explanation to anyone.

DAYA

CHAPTER 3

The History of LGBTQ+ Rights and Representation

This chapter is all about:

Positive events in LGBTQ+ history

LGBTQ+ representation and visibility

74

LGBTQ+ THROUGHOUT HISTORY

The term LGBTQ+ might be a recent development, and the fact that so many people are discussing things like this, with sexuality and gender being spoken about in such detail, is fairly new.

But the identities aren't new. The feelings aren't new. People have been living and loving all sorts of ways since the beginning of, well… people. This might surprise you, but pirates had a long history of same-sex marriage, and one of Rome's most beloved emperors was openly gay – although the term "gay" wasn't used back then. Just because they couldn't label it doesn't mean it wasn't happening. Language is evolving all the time, and we are still being introduced to new words for existing identities. There are a lot more terms to use today, and that's pretty awesome, as are the people who trailblazed their way to create social and political change and force long-overdue changes in the law to promote equality for all.

Positive social, political and legislative changes throughout LGBTQ+ history

BC to AD

630BC

Men in Cretan society form lifelong romantic relationships with other men that are recognized by society.

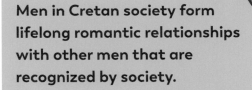

Roman Emperor Trajan takes the throne. He is one of Rome's most beloved emperors and openly gay.

AD98

27BC

The first recorded same-sex marriage takes place in the Roman Empire, under the reign of Augustus.

Marriage between male pirates, called matelotage, after the French word for sailor, matelot, is common. (This is where the term "matey" originated.)

Affrèrement contracts are drawn up in France – domestic contracts built around cohabitation in which two men swear to share "one bread, one wine and one purse".

1400s

1600s

1593

Christopher Marlowe writes *Edward II*, a historical play about England's alleged gay king and his lover, Piers Gaveston. One particular passage lists historical and fictional lovers such as Alexander the Great.

Mother Clap's Molly House in London, a sort of inn or tavern where gay men were welcome to rent a bed to share with their lovers, is raided.

love

1726

1632

Queen Christina is crowned in Sweden. Known at the time for her androgyny, she is romantically involved with both men and women.

In New England, USA, the term "Boston Marriage" is coined, which refers to two women who live together without financial support from a man.

1800s

1880s

The Hundred Guineas Club in London opens, a place where gay men can safely bring their partners. The entrance fee, not surprisingly: one hundred guineas (around $10,000 today – an exclusive crowd).

love

In Germany, Lili Elbe is one of the first trans people to undergo sex reassignment surgery – now referred to as gender confirmation surgery.

1930

1948

Alfred Kinsey, biologist and sexologist, publishes the Kinsey scale, which portrays physical attraction on a scale. This revolutionized thinking on sexuality: sexual attraction had previously been thought to be fixed and binary – either heterosexual or homosexual.

81

In the UK, The Sexual Offences Act decriminalizes homosexual activity for males aged over 21.

1967

1969

After years of violent raids by the police, customers at the gay bar Stonewall Inn in New York City fight back, refusing to be arrested. The clash runs long into the night. As we now know, this is a pivotal moment for the Pride movement.

love

The rainbow flag is unveiled at the San Francisco Gay and Lesbian Freedom Day Parade, designed by San Franciscan artist Gilbert Baker. It becomes the symbol for the Pride movement.

1978

1988

Section 28 of the Local Government Act is introduced in the UK under Prime Minister Margaret Thatcher. It prohibits any kind of promotion and/or portrayal of homosexuality by local authorities. Its impact was mostly felt in schools, where LGBTQ+ children had no access to support.

The twenty-first century

The ban on serving in the military is lifted for members of the LGBTQ+ community in the UK.

The Gender Recognition Act is passed in the UK, which legally allows transgender people to identify with their chosen gender, as well as acquire a new birth certificate.

2000   **2004**

2003   **2010**

Section 28 is repealed in England, Wales and Northern Ireland.

The US policy of "Don't Ask, Don't Tell" for LGBTQ+ individuals serving in the military is lifted.

The Marriage (Same-Sex Couples) Act comes into effect in England and Wales, finally making same-sex marriage legal. Scotland follows suit later in the same year.

The USA legalizes same-sex marriage across all states of America.

Australia legalizes same-sex marriage.

2014 2015

2018

2017

2019

In the UK, the "Turing Law" (formally the Policing and Crime Act 2017) is passed to introduce a statutory pardon for men convicted historically because of their sexuality.

The World Health Organization declassifies transgender health issues as a mental illness.

Same-sex marriage is legalized in Northern Ireland.

REPRESENTATION AND VISIBILITY

It's important that there are positive representations of the LGBTQ+ community across society and the media. When members of the community see themselves authentically represented on screen and stage and in books, it improves their self-worth and self-esteem. Accepting and inclusive fictional worlds in which queer people exist not only provide hope and joy to LGBTQ+ individuals, they also allow cis people to better understand queer identities, which helps build understanding and acceptance.

Media representation and visibility

The GLAAD "Where We Are on TV" report (2021–22) records an increase in the amount of LGBTQ+ regular series characters on TV over the last ten years, from 3 per cent in 2011–12 to 11.9 per cent in 2021–22. A total of 141 series with regular and recurring LGBTQ+ characters appeared on TV in 2022, such as Nick and Charlie in the Netflix series *Heartstopper*.

> **I know from growing up and not seeing characters that looked like me, how invisible it made me feel.**
>
> **Gloria Calderón Kellett**

TV SHOWS, FILMS, BOOKS AND VIDEO GAMES

TV shows

Representation for the LGBTQ+ community on television has never been better. Here are a sample of family-friendly TV shows with queer representation:

- *Steven Universe* (2013) (rated PG)
- *The Fosters* (2013) (rated TV-14)
- *Atypical* (2017) (rated TV-14)
- *She-Ra and the Princesses of Power* (2018) (rated TV-Y7-FV)
- *Kipo and the Age of Wonderbeasts* (2020) (rated PG)
- *The Owl House* (2020) (rated TV-Y7-FV)
- *Heartstopper* (2022) (rated 12)
- *First Kill* (2022) (rated TV-MA)

Films

The Disney film *Strange World* (2022) features Ethan Clade, the first gay lead character in a Disney animated film. Ethan Clade is voiced by gay comedian Jaboukie Young-White. Other family-friendly films with LGBTQ+ representation include:

- *Breakfast With Scot* (2007) (rated PG-13*)
- *Tallulah* (2016) (rated PG-13)
- *In a Heartbeat* (2017) (rated TV-PG)
- *Love, Simon* (2018) (rated PG-13)
- *The Most Dangerous Year* (2018) (rated 12+)
- *Freak Show* (2018) (rated 13+)
- *Sweetheart Dancers* (2019) (rated TV-PG)
- *The Half of It* (2020) (rated PG-13)
- *Out* (2020) (rated PG)
- *Tyler* (2021) (this film is not rated)
- *Rosaline* (2022) (rated PG-13)

Books

In recent years, a number of books with LGBTQ+ visibility have been published, focussing on authentic LGBTQ+ narratives. Books such as the *Noah Can't Even* series by Simon James Green and *Jamie* by L. D. Lapinski feature LGBTQ+ young people and are written by LGBTQ+ authors.

- *The Last Firefox* by Lee Newbery and Laura Catalán (8–12)

- *Death in the Spotlight* by Robin Stevens (9–12)

- *Magnus Chase and The Hammer of Thor* by Rick Riordan (9–12)

- *Undercover Princess* by Connie Glynn (9–12)

- *Max Kowalski Didn't Mean It* by Susie Day (9–12)

- *To Night Owl From Dogfish* by Meg Wolitzer and Holly Goldberg Sloan (10+)

- *Zenobia July* by Lisa Bunker (10+)

- *The Whispers* and *Middle School's a*

Drag, You Better Werk! by Greg Howard (10+)

 *George (Melissa's Story)* by Alex Gino (10+)

Jamie by L. D. Lapinski (10+)

Noah Can't Even, Noah Could Never and Noah Goes Nuclear by Simon James Green (10+)

Love Frankie by Jacqueline Wilson and Nick Sharratt (11+)

Girl Hearts Girl by Lucy Sutcliffe (12+)

Alex As Well by Alyssa Brugman (12+)

Heartstopper by Alice Oseman (12+)

Simon vs. the Homo Sapiens Agenda by Becky Abertalli (13+)

Video games

Gaming is mirroring the increased LGBTQ+ visibility in TV and film, and this representation is not only making games more enjoyable for LGBTQ+ players but also helping gamers explore their queerness in safe, virtual spaces. Today's gaming enables users to create LGBTQ+ characters to represent themselves. In 2020, *Tell Me Why* (16+) was widely recognized as the first AAA video game to feature a transgender lead character. Other video games that include queer representation are:

- *Celeste* (age 10+)
- *Hollow Knight* (age 10+)
- *Stardew Valley* (age 10+)
- *Outer Wilds* (age 12+)
- *Fire Emblem Fates* (age 13+)
- *Granblue Fantasy: Versus* (age 13+)
- *Kitty Powers' Love Life* (age 13+)

- *Phoenix Wright: Ace Attorney – Trials and Tribulations* (age 13+)
- *Scott Pilgrim vs. the World: The Game – Complete Edition* (age 13+)
- *Octopath Traveler* (age 13+)

CHAPTER 4

Game Changers, Key Figures and Icons

This chapter is all about:

Celebrating the achievements of LGBTQ+ people across history

Getting to know historical LGBTQ+ icons and twenty-first-century game changers

Exploring everyday advocates and activists

HISTORICAL GAME CHANGERS

Let's have a look at some of the most influential people across queer history – some you will have heard of or know well, and some might be new to you, but what they all have in common is that they refused to be anything other than themselves. These game changers were brave and brilliant, and at a time when society was a LOT less accepting of difference, these people refused to take no for an answer and they demanded to be heard. It's a good job they did, otherwise many freedoms we take for granted today may not even exist. So, it's time to shine the spotlight on them and celebrate their difference and the difference they made.

not a phase

We have to be visible. We are not ashamed of who we are.

SYLVIA RIVERA

Oscar Wilde (1854–1900)

Although he never came out as gay, Oscar Wilde is one of the most influential queer figures in history. He was a brilliant Irish writer and poet. However, when passages from his book *The Picture of Dorian Gray* were published in a magazine in 1890, they were criticized for hinting towards homosexuality. After a legal battle, where his writing – both public and private – was used against him, he was charged with "gross indecency" and imprisoned. After his release from prison, Wilde reunited briefly with his partner, Douglas, before they were forced to separate, when their families threatened to cut them off financially if they continued their relationship. More than 100 years after his death, Wilde was pardoned under the Alan Turing law (see page 101).

Pardon

To release (an offender) from the legal consequences (and blame) of an offence or conviction.

Lili Elbe (1882–1931)

Lili Elbe was a Danish painter and transgender woman, and one of the first known people in the world to undergo sex reassignment surgery. Einar Wegener (Lili's name prior to adopting Lili) first wore women's clothes when she stood in for a model and sat for a painting by Gerda Gottlieb (who later became Lili's wife). Wegener then began to dress as a woman publicly (saying she was Gerda's sister), and when they moved to Paris in 1912, she chose to identify as a woman. However, she was uncomfortable in a body that did not reflect her gender, so when she met German doctor Magnus Hirschfeld (the first doctor to study transgender lives), Lili underwent years of experimental surgery. The law in Denmark recognized Elbe's identity as a woman in 1933.

Transition
The process someone takes (with or without medical intervention) to move on from their gender assigned at birth to the gender they identify with.

Marlene Dietrich (1901–1992)

Marlene Dietrich rose to fame in the 1920s Berlin cabaret scene, an era known for its freedom and gender expression. Although married, she was known as a *garçonne*, a woman who pursued whomever she liked regardless of their gender. Her early German film roles reflected these origins, and she was often cast as a dangerous woman or femme fatale who performed in a club. However, when she went to Hollywood, Dietrich softened her image for American audiences, but she still maintained her androgynous glamour. Her 1930s film *Morocco* is infamous for one of the earliest lesbian kisses. Although she was never truly "out" to the public, she was known for her affairs with both men and women.

Alan Turing (1912–1954)

It is safe to say that the world would not be as it is today without Alan Turing. Gifted in mathematics, Turing published several significant computing papers as a student in his early twenties. He advanced the thinking on computers by exploring their limitations and how they could work (modern machines that follow the algorithms he created are now called Turing machines). During World War Two, Turing worked at Bletchley Park, where he developed a system to decrypt encoded German messages from the "unbreakable" Enigma machine that helped end the war. He continued to make mathematical breakthroughs, and his work on Artificial Intelligence defines how we think of AI today – the test used to determine whether a computer is "thinking" is called the Turing Test. Following a burglary at his house in 1952, the police learned Turing had been in a relationship with a man, and he was arrested and convicted for "gross indecency". Sadly, he took his own life a few years after.

Harvey Milk (1930–1978)

Harvey Milk is one of the best-known early LGBTQ+ political pioneers in the USA. Milk was elected to the San Francisco Board of Supervisors in 1977. Throughout his political career, he threw his weight and political power behind several historically important LGBTQ+ causes. Most notably, he sponsored a bill that outlawed discrimination based on sexual orientation, and it was one of the strongest pro-LGBTQ+ legislations in the nation. Milk also successfully campaigned against a proposed Californian law that would have banned any LGBTQ+ people from working in public schools. Tragically, he was assassinated in 1978, but he left behind a legacy that raised the visibility of queer people and gave them a voice to speak in unison.

Freddie Mercury (1946–1991)

Mercury was the frontman and lead singer of rock band Queen, considered one of the greatest stadium rock bands of all time. Mercury's flamboyant on-stage persona was crucial to the band's success, whose famous hits include "Bohemian Rhapsody" and "We Are the Champions". He enjoyed a brief romantic relationship with Mary Austin; however, the majority of his relationships were with men. Mercury's sexuality was often debated and journalists tried to "out" him, but he felt no need to explain his lifestyle. By never hiding his authentic self and refusing to justify his sexuality, he became an LGBTQ+ inspiration (at a time when homosexuality had only recently been decriminalized). Tragically, Mercury was a victim of the late-twentieth-century AIDS crisis, dying aged 45 of AIDS-related illness, but not before he showed the world that being queer was nothing to be ashamed of.

Sylvia Rivera (1951–2002)

Sylvia Rivera lived openly as a trans woman and fought all her life for her rights and the rights of others. She was one of the LGBTQ+ people at the Stonewall Inn who fought back on the night of the riots, and she helped organize the subsequent Christopher Street Liberation Day parade (that later became Gay Pride). She founded STAR (Street Transvestite Action Revolutionaries), a shelter for homeless trans teens, with Marsha P. Johnson (another queer game changer). She campaigned within the queer community for the inclusion of trans people; her famous speech at the 1973 Christopher Street Liberation Day rally highlighted the battle trans people were facing to get any support from the queer community. To this day, her bravery in the Stonewall uprising still inspires LGBTQ+ activists around the world.

RuPaul Charles (1960–present)

RuPaul Charles worked on the Atlanta club scene in the early 1990s as an androgynous drag artist, but his massive club hit "Supermodel (You Better Work)" in 1993 launched Charles to unprecedented levels of fame for a drag queen. Having ditched the androgyny for full glamour, he gained a modelling contract with MAC Cosmetics, his own talk show on MTV and played bit parts in films. In 2009, he created the iconic *RuPaul's Drag Race*, which has launched the global career of hundreds of drag artists and inspired several drag conventions. Ironically, after having famously said "Drag will never be mainstream", Mama Ru is responsible for having made drag a global sensation and provided a platform for a whole new generation of drag queens who continue to further discussions on gender.

Alison Bechdel (1960–present)

Alison Bechdel is a writer and illustrator whose first memoir, *Fun Home*, was written about the experience of accepting her sexuality at the same time as realizing her dad was gay. She is best known for co-creating the Bechdel-Wallace test (sometimes known as the Bechdel Test) with her friend Liz Wallace. This test is a quick way to work out whether a film has even entry-level representation of female characters, and it must pass three criteria: are there at least two female characters, are they both named and do they share a conversation about something other than a man? The test was first presented as a strip in her comic *Dykes to Watch Out For*, and the strip itself, which has run since the 1980s, is essential queer culture reading.

Booan Temple
(DOB unknown–present)

Booan Temple has mostly managed to avoid fame, but her influence and impact on queer history cannot be underestimated. In 1988 in the UK, Section 28 of the Local Government Act forbade local authorities and educational institutions from "promoting" homosexuality. Temple recognized the danger this posed to an already vulnerable LGBTQ+ community (the UK was a hostile environment post the AIDS crisis) as it would remove any education about LGBTQ+ issues, and queer youth would have no resources to educate themselves on queer identities. Although protest groups formed, they were not getting enough coverage to make an impact. So, in 1988, Temple and other lesbian activists stormed the BBC Television Centre studio during a live news broadcast. One member handcuffed herself to a camera, and Temple shouted "Stop Section 28". The protest gained huge media coverage and empowered young LGBTQ+ people. Section 28 was finally revoked in 2003, but without Booan Temple it might still be around today.

Laverne Cox (1972–present)

Laverne Cox was the first out trans woman to appear on a reality show, *I Want to Work for Diddy*, and the show won a GLAAD award (GLAAD is an LGBTQ+ company that monitors LGBTQ+ representation in the media) for Outstanding Reality Series. Although she didn't win, she was so successful that she went on to produce and star in *TRANSform Me*, a reality show where trans women gave makeover advice to cis women. Laverne then went on to play trans woman Sophia Burset in Netflix's hit prison dramedy *Orange is the New Black* and she was nominated for an Emmy for the role. She was also the first openly trans person to appear on the cover of *TIME*. Cox is continually raising the profile of successful trans people in the US, and thanks to her, the conversation on transgender lives and experiences has become more prominent.

MODERN-DAY GAME CHANGERS

So, listen up...! According to recent research, Generation Z is the queerest generation ever. Almost 16 per cent of Gen Z-ers in America identify as being queer or trans. The queer generation are loud and proud, and this rise is on full display, especially with "trans realness" and young trans kids talking about their rights on queer TikTok. From designers developing fashion trends for queer bodies to celebrities painting a rainbow picture of what it means to be young, queer and famous today, this generation are redefining what it means to be human through the lens of queerness, not just for Gen Z, but for everyone else too. Phew! So, who are this new generation, what do they do and what have they achieved?

Everyone
should just
be who they
want to be.

HARRY STYLES

Alok Vaid-Menon
(1991–present)

Vaid-Menon identifies as gender non-conforming and transfeminine. They believe that "traditional expectations associated with binary gender labels hurt everyone, not just transgender people, and these fixed ideas of what it means to be a man or a woman make it difficult for people to find out who they truly are". As an internationally acclaimed author, poet, comedian and public speaker, and as a mixed-media artist, Vaid-Menon uses their work to explore themes of trauma, belonging, and the human condition, and aims to redefine beauty standards, examine colonialism and explore fluid identity. Vaid-Menon said of their book, *Beyond the Gender Binary*, "It challenges not only the binary between male, female, man and woman, but between us and them."

Their awesome achievements:

 Author of Femme in Public (2017), *Beyond the Gender Binary* (2020) and *Your Wound/My Garden* (2021)

 Appeared on HBO's *The Trans List* (2016) and *Random Acts of Flyness* (2018) and Netflix's *Getting Curious with Jonathan Van Ness* (2022)

 Creator of #DeGenderFashion, a movement to degender fashion and beauty industries.

"I believed that about myself for the bulk of my childhood – I was too much, too feminine, too hairy, too brown. I have been the cruellest person to myself."

Miley Cyrus (1992–present)

Miley Ray Cyrus (born Destiny Hope Cyrus) is an American singer, songwriter and actor who emerged as a teen idol playing the Disney Channel character Hannah Montana (2006–2011). Regarded as a successful child-actor-turned-singer, Miley has had a host of US top ten-charting singles. In 2020, she was awarded Diamond certification for "Party in the U.S.A.", recognizing sales of ten million for the single. Miley is a long-time LGBTQ+ advocate, coming out as pansexual in 2015. She made it clear that although she was in a heterosexual relationship, she still identifies as queer. She also describes her gender as being unassigned and says once she understood her gender more, she understood her sexuality more. "I was like, 'Oh – that's why I don't feel straight and I don't feel gay. It's because I'm not.'"

Their awesome achievements:

 Attained the most US Billboard 200 top-five albums in the twenty-first century by a female artist, with a total of thirteen entries

Made appearances in the animated film *Bolt* (2008) and the feature films *Hannah Montana: The Movie* (2009) and *The Last Song* (2010) and starred in the Netflix series *Black Mirror* (2019)

 Founded the non-profit Happy Hippie Foundation in late 2014 focusing on youth homelessness and the LGBTQ+ community

"My whole life, I didn't understand my own gender and my own sexuality. I always hated the word bisexual because that's even putting me in a box. I don't ever think about someone being a boy or someone being a girl."

Bretman Rock (1998–present)

Bretman Rock first rose to fame in 2015 after his contouring videos went viral on Vine, and he continued to increase his influencer status by posting comedy, cooking, fashion and workout videos on TikTok. He calls himself a digital celebrity and is an influential member of a digital generation working to challenge conversations surrounding masculinity, beauty and culture. His online presence has resulted in brand deals, such as becoming the face of Nike's "Be True" Pride campaign (2021), playing New York Fashion Week cameos, and even launching his own eyewear collection. Most recently, he added MTV reality star to his resume with the network's YouTube series *MTV's Following: Bretman Rock*, confirming Rock as one of Gen Z's leading voices. From challenging gender definitions to advocating for underrepresented communities, Rock helps unravel the complexity of a multi-layered identity in today's culture.

Their awesome achievements:

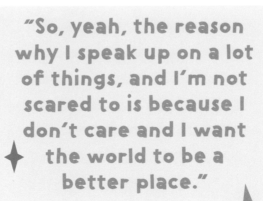

- Has won many awards, including Beauty Influencer of the Year award at People's Choice Awards (2019), Breakthrough Social Star at MTV Movie and TV Awards (2021) and Outstanding Reality Program at GLAAD Media Awards (2022)

- One of the biggest social media influencers, with nearly 20 million followers on TikTok and nine million subscribers and over 570 million views on YouTube

- Collaborated with Dime Optics to create a limited edition collection of genderless sunglasses and blue light glasses

"So, yeah, the reason why I speak up on a lot of things, and I'm not scared to is because I don't care and I want the world to be a better place."

Lil Nas X (1999–present)

Lil Nas X (born Montero Lamar Hill) is a rapper, singer, songwriter and media personality. He rose to fame following the release of country rap song "Old Town Road", and although it was initially kicked out of the country chart, it spent a record-breaking 19 weeks at the top of the singles rankings (thanks to the "Yeehaw Challenge" on TikTok). In 2012, his single, "Montero (Call Me By Your Name)", was centred around the creation of his own queer world. The video questioned what was deemed acceptable and highlighted the pressure he faced for being an openly gay artist. Lil Nas X has made art out of being unapologetically a Black gay man, redefining what it means to be a rapper, a musician and a celebrity through the lens of his queerness.

Their awesome achievements:

 The most-nominated male artist at the 62nd Annual Grammy Awards, where he won awards for Best Music Video and Best Pop Duo/Group Performance

 The first openly LGBTQ+ Black artist to win a Country Music Association award

 "Old Town Road" earned him two MTV Video Music Awards, including Song of the Year and the American Music Award for Favourite Rap/Hip Hop Song

"I know we promised to die with the secret, but this will open doors for many other queer people to simply exist."

Yasmin Finney (2003–present)

Yasmin Finney is a trans actor, best known for her role as Elle on the Netflix series *Heartstopper*, a story of queer high-school love based on the young adult graphic novel of the same name by Alice Oseman. On-screen, Yasmin plays Elle, who is living authentically and unapologetically as herself, and Yasmin says of the role, "It's about time we have young, Black queer representation on screen." Yasmin was first noticed on TikTok, where she shared her experiences of being a Black British trans woman, and she has a huge international fan base from both within the community and beyond.

Their awesome achievements:

 Often appears on "TikTok's Biggest Influencer" lists

 Received Attitude Pride Icon Award in 2022

 Played Rose in *Doctor Who* in 2023

"Hopefully, with the increase of queer-focused projects, the younger generation won't feel pressured to fit a certain mould or live up to society's expectations anymore."

You don't have to be famous to fight for LGBTQ+ rights!

Human rights are vital to protect and preserve every individual's humanity, and to ensure that every one of us can live a life of dignity and a life that is worthy of a human being.

As you know from the game changers featured in this chapter, there are many ways of fighting for and promoting LGBTQ+ rights, and we will choose different paths according to our beliefs and abilities, skills and platforms; for example, working for existing charities, organizing and signing petitions or lobbying and educating. Although they may not don capes, the following activists are just a few superheroes who have devoted themselves to the fight for justice and spoken up for tolerance and against prejudice. Pride Power!

If anyone is brave and true to themselves, it's my gay fans. The amount of confidence and fearlessness it takes to do what maybe is not what your parents expect you to do or what society may think is different – to be brave and be different and to be yourself – is just so beautiful.

BEYONCÉ

Sameer Jha

Sameer is a South Asian activist and educator. They were bullied throughout school for being different, and later came out as queer. Aged only fourteen, they used their experiences to found The Empathy Alliance, a non-profit dedicated to creating safer, more inclusive classrooms for LGBTQ+ students by training teachers about bullying. Sameer is the author of *Read This, Save Lives: A Teacher's Guide to Creating Safer Classrooms for LGBTQ+ Students* and has earned a Silver Congressional Award medal for their activism.

Avery Jackson

When Avery came out at the age of four, she and her parents decided to raise awareness about transgender children. Avery took part in a documentary called *Transhood* which platformed trans and gender nonconforming children and their lives. When she was nine, she also featured in a special issue of *National Geographic* on gender, becoming the first ever transgender person to appear on the front cover of this famous magazine. Avery's childhood experiences have helped to expand the then narrow definition of what it means to be transgender.

Sage Grace Dolan-Sandrino

Sage Grace is an Afro-Latina artist and a trained peer educator. When she transitioned at thirteen, her school community did not give her the support she needed. She decided to tell her story through the Human Rights Campaign – and became an activist. She has since been an ambassador to the White House Initiative on Advancing Educational Equity, Excellence and Economic Opportunity for Black Americans and became *Teen Vogue*'s first trans youth journalist. Sage also founded the youth creative studio and digital zine Team Mag, which is a community-based platform for other LGBTQ+ teens of colour to share resources and tell their stories.

Georgie Stone

At ten years old, Georgie became the youngest person in Australia to receive puberty blockers. She had to get permission from a court to access these, but her case led to a change in the law so that all transgender children could access puberty blockers more easily. Her activism has brought about change in safe schooling, health services and legal reform, while her presence in the media has raised awareness about the issues facing young trans people today, particularly around mental health. Georgie is best known for playing the first trans character on the Australian TV show *Neighbours*.

This world would be a whole lot better if we just made an effort to be less horrible to one another.

Elliot Page

CHAPTER 5

Practical Advice

This chapter is all about:

How you can be a game changer too

Ways to be an ally, an advocate and a friend

HOW TO BE A GAME CHANGER

Being an LGBTQ+ ally, advocate and friend is about helping to create an inclusive environment where everyone can be themselves and be treated equally and fairly within society. Any one of us, regardless of our sexual orientation and/or gender identity, can support lesbian, gay, bisexual, transgender, intersex and asexual individuals and the LGBTQ+ community. Through reading books like this one, you are already expanding your understanding of the Pride movement, basic terms and definitions and LGBTQ+ related issues, which can help you understand, support and promote positive change for the community.

This final chapter has practical suggestions on how you can be a game changer (just like the people showcased in the previous chapter) and it also includes useful resources for further information and support.

HOW TO BE A GREAT LISTENER

The BEST way to be an ally, advocate and friend is to... Be a GREAT listener.

Not all LGBTQ+ experiences are the same. Just as every LGBTQ+ person (and every person for that matter) is unique, so are their experiences. When we learn to listen well, we can really hear the specific challenges of our friends, family or peers, and only then can we learn the best way to support them. Here are some quick tips to help improve your listening skills:

Try not to jump into a conversation with your opinion. Wait for the other person to finish what they are saying.

To make sure you fully understand what the other person is saying (rather than assuming), you can rephrase what they said in your own words and ask "Did I understand that right?"

Ask questions such as, "How did that make you feel?" or "What did you learn from that experience?", which shows them you really want to understand their experience.

WAYS TO BE AN ALLY, AN ADVOCATE AND A FRIEND

Here are some things that you can do every day to create a more inclusive world:

- 💜 Believe that all people, regardless of gender identity and sexual orientation, should be treated with dignity and respect.

- 💜 Have a voice and, where you feel able to do so, speak up!

- 💜 Confront your own prejudices and unconscious bias, even if it is uncomfortable to do so (think about some of the ways discussed in Chapter 1).

- 💜 Be a listener (the tips on the previous page will help with this).

- 💜 Show respect with your language by asking new people you meet about their gender pronouns and learning vocabulary that is important to the LGBTQ+ community (flick back to Chapter 2 if you need to recap on any labels and definitions).

- Be open-minded.

- Be willing to talk.

- Be inclusive and invite LGBTQ+ friends to hang out with your friends and family.

- Don't assume that all your friends and peers are straight. Someone close to you could be looking for support in their coming-out process. Not making assumptions will give them the space they need.

- Anti-LGBTQ+ comments and jokes are harmful. Let your friends, family and peers know that you find them offensive.

- Understand LGBTQ+ issues and speak up whenever you can. By using your voice, you can have a real impact on LGBTQ+ acceptance in your community.

- Defend your LGBTQ+ friends against discrimination by calmly using information you have learned from this book or other LGBTQ+ resources.

- If you see LGBTQ+ people being misrepresented in the media, contact glaad.org to let them know.

CONCLUSION

Although the fight for equality has made significant progress over recent years, there is still so much more work to be done. We can ALL play a part in making society more welcoming for LGBTQ+ people. It is through education and knowledge that our understanding and acceptance blooms and respect and equality blossoms... allowing us ALL to flourish. The contents of this book are by no means exhaustive. It's essentially just the beginning of the road to start your own journey through queer culture, where you can follow the winding paths to the areas that interest you the most.

This book is full of pride. Pride in the key events that have shaped LGBTQ+ history. Pride in the people who have changed, and those still changing, LGBTQ+ culture. Pride in people like you who are being authentically and unapologetically themselves – and that is always the first step to a more diverse and wonderful world. How awesome is that?

You don't have
to be gay to be
a supporter –
you just have
to be a human.

DANIEL RADCLIFFE

Resources: non-fiction books

Beyond the Gender Binary by Alok Vaid-Menon

Have Pride by Grace Stewart and Sue Sanders

Here and Queer: A Queer Girl's Guide to Life by Rowan Ellis

Proud, compiled by Juno Dawson

Queerly Autistic: The Ultimate Guide for LGBTQIA+ Teens on the Spectrum by Erin Ekins

Queer Heroes: Meet 53 LGBTQ Heroes From Past and Present! by Arabelle Sicardi and Sarah Tanat-Jones

Queer Up: An Uplifting Guide to LGBTQ+ Love, Life and Mental Health by Alexis Caught

The Stonewall Riots: Coming Out in the Streets by Gayle E. Pitman

The Extraordinary Life of Alan Turing by Michael Lee Richardson and Freda Chiu

The Extraordinary Life of Freddie Mercury by Michael Lee Richardson and Maggie Cole

This Book Is Gay and What's the T?: The No-Nonsense Guide to All Things Trans and/or Non-Binary for Teens by Juno Dawson

Pride: The Story of Harvey Milk and the Rainbow Flag by Rob Sanders and Steven Salerno

Resources: Young people's forums

www.genderspectrum.org/articles/gender-spectrum-groups

www.lgbthero.org.uk/forums

www.lgbthotline.org/youthchatrooms

www.lgbtyouth.org.uk/groups-and-support/digital-support

www.qchatspace.org

www.trevorspace.org

Resources: podcasts

History is Gay, hosted by Gretchen Jones and Leigh Pfeffer

LGBTQ&A, hosted by Jeffrey Masters

Making Gay History, hosted by Eric Marcus

Qmmunity, hosted by Alexis Caught

QT: Queer Teen Podcast, hosted by Anthony Giorgio

Gender Reveal, hosted by Tuck Woodstock

Resources: charities

Asia

Taiwan Tongzhi Hotline Association www.hotline.org.tw/English/209

Oogachaga www.oogachaga.com

Australia

Equality Australia www.equalityaustralia.org.au

Pride Foundation Australia www.pridefoundation.org.au

The Equality Project www.theequalityproject.org.au

Europe

Black Trans Alliance www.blacktransalliance.org

Cassero LGBTI+ Center www.cassero.it

Ditch the Label www.ditchthelabel.org

FELGTBI+ www.felgtbi.org

Galop www.galop.org.uk

Gaysians www.gaysians.org

Gendered Intelligence www.genderedintelligence.co.uk

Hidaya www.hidayahlgbt.com

Human Dignity Trust www.humandignitytrust.org

Lambda Literary www.lambdaliterary.org

Mermaids www.mermaidsuk.org.uk

Metro www.metrocharity.org.uk

MindOut www.mindout.org.uk

Stonewall www.stonewall.org.uk

North America

Center for Black Equity www.centerforblackequity.org

Egale www.egale.ca

GLAAD www.glaad.org

Hetrick-Martin Institute www.hmi.org

LGBT Youthline www.youthline.ca

Sylvia Rivera Law Project www.srlp.org

The Attic Youth Center www.atticyouthcenter.org

The Audre Lorde Project www.alp.org

The Marsha P. Johnson Institute www.marshap.org

Trans Lifeline www.translifeline.org

Global

Human Rights Campaign Foundation www.thehrcfoundation.org

It Gets Better Project www.itgetsbetter.org

The Fund for Global Human Rights www.globalhumanrights.org/what-we-do/lgbtq-rights

Outright International www.outrightinternational.org

References

Action for Children. (2022.06.24). "*Representation Matters: Are LGBTQ+ young people seeing themselves represented in the media?*" www.actionforchildren.org.uk/blog/representation-matters-are-lgbtq-young-people-seeing-themselves-represented-in-the-media

Alexander, S. (2019). *The Little Book of Queer Icons*. Summersdale Publishers Ltd

ALOK. (n.d.). "*About*" www.alokvmenon.com/about

Booktrust. (n.d.). "*Teen and YA books with LGBT characters*". www.booktrust.org.uk/booklists/l/lgbt-ya

Bloodworth, A. (2021.04.10). "*7 Reasons Why Lil Nas X Is the LGBTQ Icon the World Needs Right Now*". Huffpost. www.huffingtonpost.co.uk/entry/lil-nas-x-lgbtq-role-model_uk_6070210bc5b6616dcd763642

Britannica Kids. (n.d.). "*Stonewall riots*". Encyclopædia Britannica. https://kids.britannica.com/students/article/Stonewall-riots/313707

Burney, O. (2020.10.14). "*Miley Cyrus, Bella Thorne, Cara Delevingne – 10 LGBT Hollywood and music stars who identify as pansexual*". Style. www.scmp.com/magazines/style/news-trends/article/3105393/miley-cyrus-bella-thorne-cara-delevigne-10-lgbt

Cheung, R. (2022.10.07). "*Bretman Rock*". The WOW. www.wowmag.co.uk/archive/bretman-rock

Clark, K. (n.d.). "*It's About Your Rights and Freedom*". Identiversity. www.identiversity.org/topics/lgbtq-identities/history-of-pride

Clark, L. (n.d.). "*Respect and acceptance of pride month*". Behavioural Health. www.childandadolescent.org/respect-and-acceptance-of-pride-month

Common Sense Media. (n.d.). "*Games With LGBTQ+ Characters*". www.commonsensemedia.org/lists/games-with-lgbtq-characters

Curtis Brown. (n.d.). "*Yasmin Finney*". www.curtisbrown.co.uk/client/yasmin-finney

Daly, R. (2022.01.02). "*Lil Nas X opens up about coming out and celebrating his sexuality*". NME. www.nme.com/news/music/lil-nas-x-opens-up-coming-out-celebrating-sexuality-3128521

Dameshenas, S. (2022.10.31) "*From* Heartstopper to Young Royals: *The best LGBTQ+ shows on Netflix*". Gay Times. www.gaytimes.co.uk/culture/the-best-lgbtq-inclusive-shows-you-can-watch-right-now-on-netflix

De Cartagena, A. (2021.06.25). "*BRETMAN ROCK IS MAKING IT CLEAR, B*TCH: SPEAK OUT, STAND UP FOR PRIDE*". Nylon. www.nylonmanila.com/bretman-rock-speak-out-stand-up-pride

Dyer, H. (2021). *The Little Book of LGBTQ+: An A–Z of Gender and Sexual Identities.* Summersdale Publishers Ltd

Dyer, H. (2019). *The Queeriodic Table: A Celebration of LGBTQ+ Culture.* Summersdale Publishers Ltd

Eatough, E. (2022.05.26). "*LGBTQ acceptance across the globe: 5 ways to encourage change*". BetterUp. www.betterup.com/blog/lgbtq-acceptance#:~:text=LGBTQ%20acceptance%20is%20critical%20for,every%20person%2C%20around%20the%20world

Heckin Unicorn. (2021.09.16). "*What is the Philadelphia People of Colour-Inclusive pride flag and what does it mean?*". https://heckinunicorn. com/blogs/heckin-unicorn-blog/what-is-the-philadelphia-people-of-colour-inclusive-pride-flag-and-what-does-it-mean

Gayety. (2022.06.07). "*Is Willow Smith bisexual and polyamorous?*". www.gayety.co/willow-smiths-sexuality

GLAAD. (n.d.). "*10 Ways to Be an Ally & a Friend*". www.glaad.org/resources/ally/2

Guha, N. (2022.0. 01). "*Why LGBTQIA+ Representation in TV Shows and Movies Is So Important—Here Are 10 to Watch as a Family*". Parents. www.parents.com/parenting/dynamics/lgbtq/why-lgbtqia-representation-tv-shows-and-movies-is-so-important

Igoe, K. (2022.04.01). "*31 Different Pride Flags and What Each Stands For*". Marie Claire www. marieclaire.com/culture/g32867826/lgbt-pride-flags-guide

Kids Helpline. (2019.10.08). "*Sexual Identity*". https://www. kidshelpline.com.au/teens/issues/sexual-identity

McNamara,B. (2019.06.27). "*Willow Smith Opened Up About Her Sexuality and Polyamory*". Teen Vogue. https://www.teenvogue.com/story/willow-smith-opened-up-about-her-sexuality-and-polyamory

Mukhtar, A. (2022.11.02) "*Yasmin Finney's Casting in* Doctor Who*? 'It Will Change The World'*". British Vogue. www.vogue.co.uk/arts-and-lifestyle/article/yasmin-finney-british-vogue-interview

Newsround. (2022.06.01). "*Pride: What is it and why do people celebrate it?*". www.bbc.co.uk/newsround/52872693

Newsround. (2022.05.20). "*Royal Mint rainbow 50p coin to celebrate 50 years of Pride*". www.bbc.co.uk/newsround/61519412

Paryrus. (n.d.). "*Why pride month is still needed*". https://www.papyrus-uk.org/why-pride-month-is-still-needed/

Peay, M. (2022.10.28). "*Lil Nas X Is A Gay Visionary That Music Needs*". Essence. www.essence.com/entertainment/only-essence/lil-nas-x-lgbtq-legacy

Pousher, J and Kent, N. (2020.06.25). "*The Global Divide on Homosexuality Persists*". www.pewresearch.org/global/2020/06/25/global-divide-on-homosexuality-persists

Sobel, A. (n.d.). "*The Complete Guide to Queer Pride Flags*". Pride. www.pride.com/pride/queer-flags

Stonewall. (n.d.). "*List of LGBTQ+ terms*". www.stonewall.org.uk/list-lgbtq-terms#:~:text=%E2%80%8BL-,Lesbian,also%20identify%20with%20this%20term

The Diversity Center of Northeast Ohio. (n.d.). "*Pronouns: A How-To*". www.diversitycenterneo.org/about-us/pronouns

Thomson Reuters. (n.d.). "*10 ways to celebrate Pride month*". https://insight.thomsonreuters.com/sea/business/posts/10-ways-to-celebrate-pride-month

TriPride. (n.d.). "*Pride Flags*". www.tripridetn.org/pride-flags

Weinberg, L. (2021.11.23). "*How Miley Cyrus Became One of the Fiercest LGBTQ+ Icons in the World*". E News. www.eonline.com/news/1283694/how-miley-cyrus-became-one-of-the-fiercest-lgbtq-icons-in-the-world

Yurcaba, J. (2021.07.29) "'*Are you ready to heal?*': Nonbinary activist Alok Vaid-Menon deconstructs gender". NBC News. www.nbcnews.com/nbc-out/out-news/are-ready-heal-nonbinary-activist-alok-vaid-menon-deconstructs-gender-rcna1544

IMAGE CREDITS

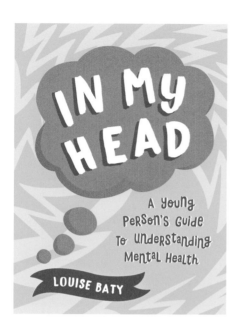

In My Head

ISBN: 9781800071957

This accessible guide for 11–15-year-olds will help young people to understand and manage their mental health.

Whether you want to understand your thoughts and emotions a little better, or learn some handy tips to help you to de-stress, it's filled with information on how to look after your well-being and stay feeling good.

In My Head will help you get to know your own mind, and give you the tools and techniques to make sure you're feeling happy and healthy.

Have you enjoyed this book?

If so, why not write a review on your favourite website?

If you're interested in finding out more about
our books, find us on Facebook at **Summersdale
Publishers**, on Twitter at **@Summersdale** and on
Instagram and TikTok at **@summersdalebooks** and
get in touch. We'd love to hear from you!

Thanks very much for buying this Summersdale book.

www.summersdale.com